THE TRASHMAN IS RICH

THE TRASHMAN IS RICH

JAVONTE' JENNINGS

authorHOUSE®

AuthorHouse™
1663 Liberty Drive
Bloomington, IN 47403
www.authorhouse.com
Phone: 1-800-839-8640

Published by AuthorHouse   11/14/2012

ISBN: 978-1-4772-3260-6 (sc)
ISBN: 978-1-4772-3259-0 (e)

Any people depicted in stock imagery provided by Thinkstock are models, and such images are being used for illustrative purposes only.
Certain stock imagery © *Thinkstock.*

This book is printed on acid-free paper.

Contents

Real Estate

Tax Liens.. 11

What is interest rates?.. 14

What is redemption? 16

Bidding Methods 17

Why Invest in Tax Liens?...................................... 20

Not so Fast! 22

Why Governments allow Tax Liens? 23

How to avoid Tax liens 24

Using your IDA, IRA or 401K to invest............... 26

Buying property before the auction 27

What happens if you invest in a property you really don't want
    to keep?.. 29

Who will look over your property if you invest in another State 31

Okay Javonte', what is Tax Deeds?........................ 34

Why don't Realtors tell people about this way to buy homes? 35

This sounds like a scam! Why should you believe me? 37

More investing! You can help people facing Foreclosure...................... 39

Communication is everything! 41

Ways to sell your properties online 42

Want to sell your property yourself? 43

Buying a property from the seller 45

Buying a property from a Realtor 47

Definitions for Real Estate.................................... 48

Car Auctions

Car Auctions 53
How to get started? 54
How do you know if these cars work? 56
What's the best way to advertise? 58
How I became a dealer 60
What's my advice 62
How many cars can you sell without paying taxes 64
Where can you get used parts from 65
Who can you get to fix your cars 67
Walking away happy 69
Definitions for Car auctions 70

Storage Auctions

Storage Auctions? 73
Bidding Methods 74
What can this investment do for you 75
Don't fill bad 76
How much time do you have to clear the unit 77
They are not your friends 78
Knowing the value of your product 80

The Millionaire dress code

The Millionaire Dress-code 83
How to purchase cloths for cheap 84
Being court off guard 85
Combinations 86
Walk to Walk 87
Writer Thoughts 89
Legal Notice Sample 91
Home Inspection Sheet 93
General Walk Through 95
Living Room 96
Dining Room 97
Den 98

Kitchen 99
Master Bedroom.. 100
Bedroom 1 101
Bedroom 2 102
Bedroom 3 103
Bedroom 4 104
Bedroom 5 105
Basement... 106
Miscellaneous.. 107
Budget Sheet 108
Car Auction Sheet 110

The Trashman is Rich is written by Javonte' Jennings. This book has not been edited by a company. The reason of me not taking that step is because I want to be able to teach people that you can be successful without a college education. As a matter of fact, I never even finished High School. But I'm very rich and wealthy because of the secrets I teach in this book. So with that being said, please accuse me for any mistakes in Grammar or Punctuation. Thank You!

Acknowledged

I would like to dedicate this book in memory of my brother Jeremy Jennings and his son Jeremy Jennings Jr who fell off a school bus in Baltimore, Md 2010. Thanks to my older brother Johnathan for teaching me how to be wise at a young age. I also would like to thank my mother for encouraging me the whole way to where I achieved to be at today. If it wasn't for her putting positive thoughts in my head to keep striving for more out of life, I don't know where I'll be right now. My mom has always told me I was going to be someone big in life, and for the most part its been happening. I came from living in the Poe Homes to investing my money into Cars, Real Estate, and Storage auctions to gain more money on my spare-time. It's just been awesome receiving profits from these investment.

I also would like to thank my godmother Barbra Davis in Maryland for teaching me how to control my anger while learning something new. She taught me how to take 10 second breather to hold my frustration in to think before I act or speak. I would like to thank most of my teachers that taught me how to read, write, and do math very well. Its just been phenomenal the whole way! I would definitely like to thank my brothers Jakeenan and Jejuan Jennings for helping me view properties in the Baltimore Maryland area when I couldn't be there to do so. I would like to thank my father for teaching me how to be cheap. That taught me how to chase after things that's cheap but can make profits. Thanks to my sister Angel. Her name has taught me to keep Faith in my plans. I would also like to thank my investment team for being my back bone. You really help me achieve many goals outside of this and I appreciate it. I couldn't even explain how happy I am of you. And I would just like to take time out to give respect for everyone that I didn't mentioned that has been in my life to help me. Thanks to the people who know who they are.

Prefaces

In this specific book I will be teaching you the greatest kept secrets of all times. These secretes only stay between the wealthy and their families. Some people may think of it as a traditional past down or something. However, other businesses such as Banks, Loan Companies, Provide Investors, etc. Use these same Real Estate and Car auction secrets to stay in the game of flipping, buying, and selling properties and cars.

You may not have known that the Banks and Dealers use these secrets and then charge you quadruple prices of what they paid for the product. That's why you will learn everything you need to know in order to build wealth, stay updated with your investment plans, and pick up on properties and cars for pennies on the dollar.

After reading this book you will be ready to enter the road of riches with ease. And you will fill good about everything that you learn and apply. Remember, you must apply the knowledge too. It's one thing to read the book, but It's another if you start right away and start receiving benefits from these investment.

I don't write books that will make you rich overnight, because I don't know of any investments that will and can do that. I simply write easy to read books that will teach you (over a matter of time) how to become rich patiently. You will learn four easy ways to pick up on Real Estate, several easy ways to pick up on Cars and other trash. First, you will learn the difference between Tax Liens and Tax Deeds. Then we will teach you how to pick the best investment plan to these properties. So read along and see how the rich stay rich. And how the poor can become rich!

What is this book about?

This book is about how to make a living in America by paying pennies on the dollar on everything you do. I grew-up in Baltimore, Maryland. When I lived in Baltimore, I didn't realize the opportunities that was there for me. If you are in the Baltimore area, then you may become the next millionaire this book teaches you to be.

I was raised around drug dealers and people that always took advantage of other people. As I got older and saw the way to a better life, I realize that a rich life is something similar to the street life. I start noticing the difference and comparison between the two. But no matter what side you're on, it's all about, "Haves and Have knots."

Being in the courthouse made me an angry young man. But check this out, the courthouse is known for many things outside of trouble. Yes, It does mean someone is in trouble with the law in some type of way, but it doesn't have to lead to jail time if you're on trash-men side of the fence. I started noticing the flip side to the courthouse. As a criminal, I wasn't paying attention. But once I got involved with this business I notice that a lot of my work have a lot to do with the court system. Now if you never been to jail, great! But for the people who I really wrote this book for, you have a chance now. I know it's hard for you to get good jobs, I know how it is when someone look at you as if you're a bad person just because of your records. But now you have an alternative when you go to the courthouse. Use this to your advantage. Be better than a job. Its plenty of things you can do to raise money instead of working a job for the rest of your life. I'm totally against that chain of command when your life have limitation on how you live. Do you want to do the rich things that can make you financially free, or do you want to keep working and not being able to do what you want or go where you want? I'm 23. I been more places across the world then most elders. Why? Because I apply the knowledge that I teach in the book.

When some people hear about awesome ways to make money, the first thing they think is that it must be some type on scam or something. Well the secrets you will learn and apply in this book will give you a better over-look of life and who to REALLY lookout for. No matter of how a person talk, look, act, respond to certain things. Always remember, that everyone on this planted is out to make money in some type of way. That's just the way of the world. Some people may not take it as serious as others, but you will notice them people by how they live.

Never take life for granted. Always invest to have nice things for your children and their children. Me, I think a little different then others when it comes to passing things down to generations under me. Because I was taught that if you can make yourself wealthy, then you can make others around you wealthy as well. Notice I said wealthy instead of Rich? Wealthy is a word used for people that knows the difference between Rich and Poor. You see, many people say they're Rich, but they don't really mean Rich as in Millions of dollars to spend on any and everything. What they mean to say is that if they cash in all their investments then they will have how much money they're claiming to have.

This rule goes for some of the famous people that you may look-up to. I know Millionaires that don't really have a lot of money, but they have a lot to claim as theirs. That's why they claim rich status. Example, lets say you have Four properties that's worth $200,000.00 a piece. Most people will tell others they're Rich because of that reason. Rich is just another word for problem solving! Once you fall in love with helping others and receiving a profit from it, then you will grow rich quicker than you think. But you have to fall in love with problem solving first because that's what brings the money in.

In the next secession you will discover a investment that can help you build wealth by helping people make their payments. If they don't make the payments by the redemption date, then you can profit in a more powerful way by taking full possession of the property. Some people may look at this investment as if you're taking advantage of people, but in all actual reality, your helping them, but if they don't obey the state laws, then you have to profit in a different way, and that way is taking ownership of the property.

The second secession you will learn all the secrets to investing in Cars. As I said before, many people may think you're taking advantage of others by bidding on their junk. Well your not! And the reason for this is because we all have to follow rules and regulations that the state provide for us. And if you choose not to follow them rules and regulations, then you lose out on your property.

The third session you will learn how to take possession of others junk by attending Storage auctions. And making extra money by selling the things that you don't want to keep.

The last session will teach you how to play the role of a Millionaire and actually live up to that standard.

Secession 1

Real Estate

The Streets

When I was 13 years of age, my brother Jeremy Jennings told me about the Tax Lien secrets before he passed away at twenty two. When he went off to Job Corps he came back a different person that had lots of knowledge on how to make money. At the time I was into the streets heavy and didn't want to take any advice from my older brother that knew about making money more than the guys that was on the streets teaching me how to make illegal money.

He watch me be a flunky for these guys for all of my juvenile life before he passed away. When I said he came back a different person, he came back sharp and intelligent! He use to have mini seminars on the block and had every drug dealer listening to the knowledge that he was speaking of.

He kept telling us that it was a such thing as penny houses and we could make money from what they call, "Tax Liens." The group of guys that he held as his listeners was also young and hustlers. We had no idea of what he was talking about because we didn't know anything about Real Estate than what he was trying to explain to us. I thought I knew a little bit about it, as far as paying a mortgage and a down payment as I was told from the elders, but he said that he knew many ways to get around that mortgage that I'd mentioned.

So one day we decide to take a trip with him down to the Municipal building located in downtown Baltimore, Maryland to listen to the clerk tell us more about the investment. When we asked him to explain to us the definition of a Tax Lien, he replied, "y'all are to young to invest!" My brother cut him off and said we would just like to know more about it for future reference. He smiled and said, "what would y'all like to know?"

3

My brother said, "everything you know." Before the clerk had a chance to speak, my brother cut him off and said, "I'm teaching them how to invest in business and they need to know all about this investment so they can be prepared as soon as we get old enough." He added "we" because he was quite young himself at the time. The clerk automatically looked at him as the leader because he knew more about the investment then any of us.

The clerk started from the beginning of what we call the W-9 form, and then he explained the bidding method, to the registration fee, along with the bidding number to bid in the auction. My brother mentioned this information too before the clerk explained it to us, but it was good to hear it again from someone in uniform.

I'm not going to lie, my mind was somewhere else because all I wanted to do was sell drugs for the quick dollar.

We stayed there for about two hours. It was more like a two man conversation with my brother and the clerk, because everyone else seemed to be spaced out as I was. The only thing I got out of it all was that you can make interest on your money if you paid someone else taxes.

My brother had got put out of Job Corps for fighting and had got sent home. One late night I asked him did they teach him the things he was teaching us in Job Corps? And he said it wasn't classwork but the teacher had experience in the business before he had became a teacher there. So in other words, the school didn't teach him this investment, but his teacher must of saw something in him to give him this knowledge. Knowing my brother, he probably asked for it. One thing I can say about him is that he always had an open eye out for making extra money outside of what he was doing.

As a couple of weeks went by and my brother came to each of us that had went with him to the Municipal building, he asked us questions to see if we was paying attention or had any interest in the new investment that he had expose to us, Like normal hoodlums, we had nothing to say but that sounds cool. We all said that! But no one took action. He wasn't looking at the fact that we was to young (15-17 years of age) he was looking to see if we had did any type of research or anything else that could have been useful to get us off the path we was following. But we didn't. No one did.

I felt a little bad because this was my brother and he knew how to do something that I didn't and I did nothing to support him.

All my life I was going in and out of jail. But when I turned 16, I had caught a serious charge that lead me to get three years in jail. I don't think it was fair for them to put it on my adult record as a juvenile, but they did anyway. (It's like they stop the children in the Brown communities from getting good jobs when they're young. Not saying the same thing don't happen in the White communities either, its just that it happen often in the Brown communities). So, a year had went past and he finally wrote me to tell me he had finally did it. He had receive some money from Social Security and he invested in Tax Liens in Baltimore. I was happy for him, but mad at myself. I had let him down many of times in my life, but I knew this had meant a lot to him from the day he first told me about it.

He had purchase Six liens. He knew that it would be a process to actually take possession of the properties, so he'd saved money to start the legal process. He was very excited about investing in this business for many reasons. He was always talking about the interest part of this business, but he also said that people will appreciate him doing them a favor by paying their taxes for a little interest on top of what he'd paid for them.

My brother also was in a gang at a early age and couldn't get out because of the consequences that it brings. I was never into that type of chain of command because I thought of it as a power thing. I guess that's why he saved me from making the same mistakes as he did. He told me that if I ever join a gang, he would break both of my arms and then tell my mother he did it. That kept me from even wanting to know how to get in it. I think that was another reason why he had took on a leadership role in our lives (the ones that was listening). He was like our leader. Not just because he was older than us, he knew more and applied it too.

After a year of being in the joint, I called home and found out that someone had killed my brother for something that involved gang activity. Someone had shot him in his home and left him there for the police to find him at the front door. I didn't know what to do at the time because I was locked-up and wasn't shore who had did it or had something to do with it. I was hurt and full of anger! Here he was on the right road to riches and someone took his life probably because they was jealous they didn't do it. That's how the life of gang bangers, drug dealers, etc, is. They hate you if you are doing the right things in life. They don't like to see you get ahead of them.

Before any of this had happen though, he had wrote me a letter telling me that he was apologizing for anything that he had done. For some reason I knew something was going on from the rhythm of the letter. It was as if he knew something was about to happen to him and he wanted to talk to me before it happen. That was the last time I talked to him.

Coming out hard

When I came home from jail it was on! I started out with a regular 9 to 5 at Burger King. I started off with just under $434.68 to invest in Tax Liens. I felt as if I owed that to my brother, to pickup where he left off at. Before I went to jail that's all he was talking about, and if I would of made it out before that happened, I know that's what he would have been influencing me to do.

I felt eager then ever to achieve this goal. I stayed on the internet for days at a time trying to find out everything I could to avoid losing my money to a gamble. I took several trips a week to the Municipal building to hear the same thing over and over again until I knew the whole speech by heart. I went there so much, they knew my name, where I lived, to the type of cloths that I like to wear.

At first they was a little up tight with me coming in there almost everyday for the same information. But after a while they got use to me asking them about Tax Liens and knew exactly what I needed to know. It got to the point where they would help me look up property records. They must of knew I was slower than others on catching on to the business. And I was!

I needed to know things that my brother didn't get a chance to teach me. And as you read this book, you will find things that you may know that I didn't mention in this book. It's not that I'm trying to keep knowledge away from you like some authors. I may not have gotten to that level of investing yet. Like when investors say they pickup on properties for no down payment. I'm not saying that they don't use this strategy, but I haven't did such thing yet, and to be completely honest, I don't think I would ever use that strategy. I like to use strategies that I have been using for years and been taught very well on how to do.

My dream is to just get enough properties to get them transported to a raw piece of land. I would like to build my own little community somewhere were my family and I can stay within our community but distance from one another. From listening to my brother's vision, I believe that was both of our dream!

From my story to your Future

"2 Dollar Bills"

Tax Liens

In order to understand what cost Tax Lien problems, we must go back to the time when the leaders put themselves in control to take over this country. When the US constitution was wrote, It was ordered that every person that owned a piece of land must pay taxes on that land to pay for the services that the state provide for that county.

To be direct, you will never own the land that your property sits on, you only own the structure. That land that your property sits on belongs to the leaders of the USA.

Tax Liens is a very simple investment. Tax Liens is when the owner of a property don't pay their taxes for the land that the home sits on. Then a lien will be held against that property (by investors) from being sold or anything else that may transfer the deed from the original owner to someone else.

The Government sets up "Tax Lien Certificate" auctions to give investors the opportunity to receive interest on there money, while given the property owners a chance to keep there homes for a little interest to the investor. It's set up for everyone to win! You can also purchase these properties before the auction occur. We'll teach you how to do that later in the book. For the most part, the counties have to make money to pay for the services, such as: Teachers, Police, Ambulance, Library, Trash companies, etc. These people get paid from the people in there states when they pay there taxes. A lot of people think the Government pay these people, but in all actual reality, these people get paid by the citizen in there counties.

So in order for the Government to pay these people, they have to put pressure on the tax payers. And property owners are one of the major tax payers.

When someone don't pay there taxes on their property, the state will advertise their property in the newspaper or auction sites several weeks before the auction. However, sometimes tax payers will pay the taxes a couple of days before the auction. Which makes them safe from their property being auctioned off. Others may not know that there properties are being advertise for sale. Some of the people that may fall a victim to this crises will be people that live out of town and have no type of interest in the property anymore. You will be surprise how many people leave there properties abandoned and just don't want anything to do with it anymore.

I have ran into many property owners that gave me a "Quick Claim Deed" without negotiating for any money. They just didn't want anything to do with it. It was that easy! Just approaching the property owner and receiving a deed that was free, that's just awesome!

When the counties start advertising the properties, you want to be the first to know about it! There will be a lot of investors that may have more money then you, so you want to be able to find the properties that fit your needs. When you find a home or investment property that interest you, you want to do what we call a "Property Record Search." This is used to see if the property have any type of liens that will interfere with your investment or interest rate. It will also stop you from investing in any properties that will cost you more money then planned. You can do this for free at the courthouse.

Now if you are a out of town investor that would like to invest somewhere you don't live, then you may have to find a loyal website that will give you all the details on that property. I must admit, there's a lot of websites that just want to take your money and will tell you anything to do just that. So you want to do a little research on that too. Remember what I said, Banks, Loan Companies, Provide Investors, and many other people with power invest in this business too, so you want to work extra hard on your research. Also keep in mind that every state offer Tax Liens, or Tax Deeds so you can invest anywhere in the USA that offers them. You don't have to invest in some of the common places that many others may know about; such as: Florida, Texas, Baltimore, or Arizona that offer high percentages on there certificates. Many small towns offer high percentages too! Never underestimate the places you don't know about.

What is interest rates?

Interest rate is when you lend someone some money (or anything that you may want more back from them) and you would like to receive more then what you'd lend them. Look at it like the Banks or Loan Companies. When you borrow money from the bank or loan companies, they charge interest because they would like to make money on that loan. That's the only way they do business!

A lot of times the interest depends on how fast you give that company or person the money back. If you pay them back fast, then the interest rate will not be that much. If you take a long time to pay them then as anything else that may have interest to it, it goes up.

Ask yourself this question. Have you ever had a dept when it was with its original company that was okay? But all of a sudden, when the dept collectors start calling your phone they start talking an outrages number? First thing you say to yourself is how did that bill get so high? Well the dept collectors pay your bill for you, and then they charge you the interest rate of their company's policy. The bill may have been just over a couple hundred dollars, but when they put their greedy hands in it, they want to receive profits that they don't even deserve. That's the same with Tax Lien interest rates, but you as the investor deserve to receive interest on your money because this is your money that you're lending to someone you will never meet. Unless you decide to purchase the property before the auction, which can be difficult at times.

Getting in contact with the owner can be a pain in the neck. And some of them don't want you to come to their house talking about you are interested in what they own. That can bring some people to a serious level of violence. Trust me, I know. More than seven times I went to approach the owner and received violent comments and behavior towards me. Its some times best to go through Uncle Sam. At least you know you are safe and you will get one or the other (your interest or the property). No doubt about that!

What is redemption?

Redemption is when someone have a specific time limit to pay you back.
This can be used for many fields outside of Tax Liens. It is most used for
when someone owe interest on an item. And you gave them a certain time
limit for them to pay you back. That's called redemption.

In Tax Liens, after the redemption period is up then you can file a complain
with the courts against the owner to take it to the next step which is called
a sheriff sale. The homeowner has up to the date of decision from the
courts to pay you back with your interest along with lawyer fees. If the
homeowner resist to pay you, then the judge will most lightly order for
the sheriff sale.

Bidding Methods

Every state require you to bid a certain way in their auctions. These is how they will conduct their auctions and there's no way around them. There's four different bidding methods. There's a "Premium Bid," This is when you will bid the highest payment that you will pay for the certificate. Example, if the lien amount was $1,829. 43. Then you will bid up the amount of the lien to how much you are willing to pay for it. It's like the most common way people know how to bid when it comes down to any type of auction. You will not be paid for the amount you've bid over the lien amount. Premium bidding means that you will pay the lien amount and then extra money to actually win the certificate. Let me put it in a better example for you. Lets say you plan on paying the lien amount (which is 1,829.43). Then the bid will start at 1,830.43 because that will be the money paid on top of the lien amount. Be careful because you can bite yourself in the leg with spending over the lien amount, remember that that money don't get paid back. That money goes to the state for the conduction of the auction. But if your interest builds up then it will override the amount you paid over the lien amount, but still be careful because you want to receive as much interest as you can on your money.

The opposite bidding method is called "Bid Down" method. This is when you are bidding down the interest rate you are willing to accept. Example, say if the lien amount was $721.90. Then you will be bidding down the interest rate you are willing to receive on that $721.90. Make sense? Lets say your state offers 16 percent on their certificates, then you will be bidding down the 16 percent interest rate to what you are willing to take until one of your components gives in. So you will still pay the $721.90, but the interest rate will change because that's what you're bidding on.

Now the "Rotation Bid" is not very polar, however it is used in some counties. This is when the county gives every participant a chance to bid on the property. Meaning they will go around the room in seating order to see if the bidder would like to purchase the lien. Some people may not get a chance to bid on the property. My advice to you if you are participating in a Rotation bidding method, is to have more then one person with you to obtain the lien you are interested in.

The next bidding method is called "Random Bid," this is when the auctioneer (or whom ever handling the sale) pick a random bidder and gives them the opportunity to purchase the lien. This one is used very seldom.

The counties also offer what they call (OTC) over the counter liens. This is when you will not have to bid in the auction, you can simply go to the county and ask them for the list of properties that was not sold in the auction. Many counties do this on their online websites.

They will provide a bundle (list) of properties for you to fill out a form for the ones you will like to purchase and give them a cashiers check or use your debit card for all the lien amounts. Then they make sure your funds went through without any problems. Finally, they will put your name in the computer as the lien holder. Make sure to get a receipt back. Usually, if done online, they mail your receipt back to your email address. That's conformation that you did purchase them.

Now, the amazing part about this type of bidding is that you receive EVERY penny on your interest rate. Lets say the state offers 24% on their Certificates, then you receive every penny of that if the lien is paid off. AND! There is no competition in this technique. So you don't have to compete with anyone for the certificate. That's great in my eyes! Secret from me to you, this is the best way to invest in Tax Liens. Because you are protecting yourself by gaining all the interest on your money that that state offers.

Most states have leftover certificates from years and years ago. Because Tax Liens is a secretive investment, many people (besides the ones that's been involved sense God knows when) don't know about them. You should get on the phone right now and ask your county if they have any leftover certificates that haven't been sold in the auction. Nine times out of ten, they will. Now some counties won't sell them to you until there auction arrives. And this can be once every year, or as many times as once every month.

Now when the thought of writing this book came to my mind, I promise myself to give you all of my secrets along with other investors I know. So with that being said, I will teach a very useful secret that me and a investing buddy of mines used that build us unbelievable wealth. If we are looking to own a property, then we would look for properties that have a slight chance of being redeemed. Like properties with the lien amount so high, that we know the property owner will not have the money to pay it back in the period of time that's giving by the state.

If we just want to make a quick profit on our money, then we will bid on small liens that will most lightly get paid off quick by the loan and mortgage companies. But large lien amounts may not get pay off that quick, or may never get paid off being as though its gaining interest every day you hold that certificate.

Another example, lets say you have a property that you are really interested in purchasing, and the amount of the lien is $12,953.50 There's a strong possibility that that lien will not get paid off. And you may become the new owner of that property. As a $149.00 lien amount may get paid off in a month or so. That's the difference between the bidding strategies. You want to find the best strategies that fits your needs. In order to do that, you have to know rather or not you would like to keep the property or gain interest on your money.

Why Invest in Tax Liens?

I have been involved in Tax Liens since 2009. When I first got involved in Tax Liens, I had just got out of jail. Over the months of 2009, I studied every day until I was certain about were my money would be going. I did realize this was a waiting game for the outcome. So I just took a chance and invested in a auction in Mohave, Arizona. I choose Arizona because I never been west so I decide to invest in this side of the coast to live on. The lien was redeemed eight months later with the interest rate of 8%.

At the time it didn't seem like much, but as I started doing it more often, it hit me that this was not a get rich over night scam. It takes time! But, If you use some of the bidding strategies that was mentioned earlier in the bidding chapter, then you will be able to avoid some of the down falls and manifest a proper investment plan that will fit your needs.

Why invest in Tax Liens? Because Tax Liens is better than keeping your money in the banks. Think about it. When you keep your hard earned money in the banks, they want to charge you for holding your money, transferring, transactions, and using the ATM machines. They make more money off you then you can imagine! With Tax Liens, you are keeping your money in a safe place and you receive INTEREST on your money, instead of being taxed for your money. Make sense? Of course it does!

The worse thing that can happen (that is also a good thing in this business) is that you end up with the property. And that's still a great thing! Me personally, I rather take my chances investing in myself, and make money. Then being taken advantage of by someone that I know won't help me out If I needed it the most. Banks and rental offices are not like human beings. They won't help you for any reason. They have a business to run, and as we all know by now, they are not negotiable when it comes down to people owing them money.

Let me be more specific, let me use a foreclosure property as an example. Lets say you just lost your job because the economy had a hard down turn. Banks want their money no matter how things look for you. They either get their payments or they take their home back from you when the time line is up. And then sell it to someone else for the same price you saw it on the market for. You see? They are taking back their property and then put it back on the market for the same price they was going to sell it to you for. You may have put a down payment of $50,000.00 for a $125,000.00 home. Meaning, you only owe a $75,000 thousand more. But they turn around and put it back on the market for the full $125,000.00. Now if that's not getting over on folks, then I don't know what is.

How can you do that? How can you make $50,000.00 off one person and then turn around and make the other $125,000.00 off someone else? And that's if they don't go through the same crisis as you. Only banks! If your going to make that much of a gamble, just do the right thing by investing in yourself. That way you are in full control of your investment. Don't make yourself comfortable with the power in someone else or companies hands.

Please don't make these same mistakes I watch some of my family and friends do. After reading this book, you should be well aware of the mistakes to avoid.

Not so Fast!

Now when you are at the point to where as though you have not receive your redemption back, then you have to go through one more process before taking procession of the property. This may get your mind thinking a little, but its well worth it and I'm going to explain why.

If the Tax Lien certificate has not been redeemed, the certificate holder cannot institute foreclosure and receive the deed; a public deed sale must occur. This is when you are still the lien holder, but you still have to go through a second bid to see if anyone else will like to purchase the lien with the interest you gained on top of it. So in other words, lets say that your lien and interest all in one is $1,267.90 then you will have that amount already up on the bidders that want to bid on the property. So when they bid on the property, they are actually going to pay the redemption payment that the owner was going to pay you (or suppose to pay you). And if you still want the property from that point on, then you will just bid on it. But remember that you still have the amount that you put in the lien already in the bid. Do you fully understand?

Okay, lets use another example. Lets say I invested in a certificate and I put $2,308.00 into it. That's including the lien amount, how much interest the owner owe me, and the fees my lawyer charged me for the legal process. If the owner doesn't redeem the property back from me for what ever reason, then when I attend the second auction to take full possession of the property, I will have that same amount up on the table to bid off if things go over that amount.

Why Governments allow Tax Liens?

The Government allow Tax Liens because its a win win investment for both, the investor and the person that's in crisis. See, as mentioned in previous chapters, the state have to pay for the services that they provide for the US citizens. The Government receives the Taxes they need to pay for the services. The investors receive interest on his/her money. And the homeowners gets to keep their homes.

The investment speaks for itself. At one point of time, you had to actually go to the courthouse to bid on these properties. That was before my time thank the Lord. Now since the computer has become a major glitch to the American lifestyle, you can go online to bid on these properties. Which makes it very easier as a home base business.

Some people sit there and talk bad about the Government and the things that they are entitled to do, but if you do your homework on the beneficial things that they stamp, you will see they're not bad people at all. You just have to find out what side you're going to choose from them when it comes down to being Poor or Rich.

Have you ever saw the movie Little Giants? Did you studied the movie cover? Well look closely and you will notice that its an offense and defense side. The defense is dress all the same, the offense is dress all different. Me personally, I look at the secrets in little things like that, that tells me a lot about what side I choose from the Government.

You can be depress by going through the banks and having to make a payment every paycheck (If you have a job the whole time as your contract), or you can buy your own properties that can set you stress free. The bottom line is the choice is yours! Just be smart and think rational.

How to avoid Tax liens

Now for me to flip this book from a profit to a Prophet is abnormal to some people. But I was always taught to help people rise mentally while making money at the same time. Helping people become righteous people always been my dream. The same way I teach you how you can make money from this investment, I have to teach the people that face these crises how to avoid Tax Liens.

Now when you are in this type of situation, it's not a fun experience, We are talking about losing something you own forever. So to avoid a Tax Lien on your property, what you want to do is get into a routine of saving your money for life saving matters like this. Not only do you want to save your money, but you also want to collect as much knowledge as you can on home-ownership. You may think owning a home is a easy thing to do, and it is! If you are looking into making an living out of renting your current home to buy more. That can open up doors for you to build residual income for early retirement.

Think of it like this, you want to retire early if you can. Never look towards working for the rest of your life or to an age you may not make it to. If you already own a home then you are in the best position because you can move on to a better lifestyle by investing in more then what you already have. This especially goes for if you don't have a mortgage to pay every month. Wipe the sweat off your heads now, because you're in an excellent position to do what will be best for you to build an stable foundation for your family. You only live once, but remember everything you do effect your next generation. So you want to build that foundation for them, so they can avoid some of the mistakes you made.

I don't know about you, but I want my children children to be Rich when they come into this world. Like the movie Richie Rich. That child was already rich before he was considered a child. His father build that foundation for him to come into. That's great! And not impossible to do if you start right away. In the back of the book you will have a budget sheet that will help you save your money if you apply it in your investment plan. This will help you avoid getting into any type of insurance or Tax Lien problems. This should keep you on the right track to saving money for things like this.

Using your IDA, IRA or 401K to invest

IDA (Individual Development Account) is a program that allows you to save money to be matched at the end of the program. It's a two years savings program, but after the first year of saving, you can withdraw the cash. For the year of 2012, they are matching $4,500.00 to your $1,500.00. So that's $6000.00 cash you have after the two years of saving to invest in a business, go back to school, put down for a down payment on your first home or pay towards your home you're already living in. When you save money through the program, they will match it with a greater amount. Its a legit company through the "Federal Funding" system so you don't have to worry about being taking advantage of. Also to verify anything that I say, just check with the "Better Business Bureau," they have the right data to verify the program is legit.

The Government also allow you to use your 401K and IRA to invest in Tax Liens without any penalties. I'm not a big knowledgeable person when it comes down to this subject because I don't know much about either two. But from what I've been taught, you can invest from these to beneficiary programs.

To find out more information on how to invest from your 401K or IRA, you may want to take a visit to your local Municipal building or better yet, talk to your IRA Or 401K planner to find out the proper way to invest from these accounts.

Buying property before the auction

You can purchase the home from the homeowner before the auction. Did you know that? What you want to do is be the first to know about whose property is going up for sale in the ads. Once you discover your target, then you want to know exactly who you're looking for and what you are looking for. That's including their name, address, the lien amount, how many people is on the deed, and anything else you may think of that wasn't mentioned. This is one of those processes that may or may not go as you planned or want it to go.

When people are facing losing their home, they can get upset with others for no apparent reason. So you want to be smooth about how you approach them. You can always write a letter to inform them that you saw their property in the newspaper or the website being advertise for sale in the next auction, and that you would like to buy their property from them before it gets auctioned off.

Now this can be the best way to approach someone when they're facing these situations, because they can contact you if they are interested in your interest in the property. Make sure to leave them your name, a phone you can be reached at, fax numbers, or email address. You want to leave this information with them for contact purposes. I lost out a few times from being afraid to give people this information because I didn't want to offend them, but after communicating with other investors, I found out that this can be the best information to leave them just encase they do want to sell.

Like I said before some people don't want anything to do with the properties they own. I know it may sounds crazy but it happens like that sometimes.

Its like they are not worried about it if they already have somewhere to live. I really don't know how to explain it, you just have to go out and see for yourself to see what I'm talking about. When someone tell you something, it's nothing like experiencing it for yourself. When you pickup on these properties you'll take all the credit for yourself of course, but just remember to teach others. Don't be greedy because its plenty of properties for you to pickup the same way.

What happens if you invest in a property you really don't want to keep?

When you buy a property that you later on down the line realize you would not like to keep, its plenty of things you can do with these properties. The first thing that comes to most investors mind is to sell right away. Well, for an investor such as myself, I know the Tax laws quite well and I would simply donate the property to a organization or church to receive a Tax write off. If you use this technique, you may not have to pay taxes (up to a percentage) for that year.

Or you can always use the property for renting or selling purposes. It's really numerous of things you can do with this question. And I can only tell you but so much. You may want to consider one of the above strategies to this question. I don't consider selling properties, so I don't speak much about that.

If I invest in a property, it's because I want to rent, live, or donate it to a homeless family. That's why I invest in this business. But, as in any type of business, everyone will have there own purpose. My mother always taught me to use my mind to invest, but also have a heart for people too. Meaning, if you see someone that needs a place to stay, help them out for a couple of months until they get themselves together. Now, I didn't say be a fool! But if you're holding onto a property that you are not renting out, why not help someone else out? One thing I learned in this little world, is that you never know who may become that overnight Millionaire, so just be careful how you treat people.

Also, owing property can be a hassle at times. There are going to be many times where you won't fill the need to hold onto certain properties and just want to give them away for a low cost. I met many investors in this business that often find low income families to help them out. When I say help them out, what I mean to say is that they pay the insurance and taxes on the property each year to have a home to stay in for there low income budgets.

Think about it, you are purchasing Real Estate for pennies on the dollar, so in some cases you can afford to help someone else out, in some cases.

Just know that you are an investor that would like to build business for the future, so doing someone else a huge favor like that can draw many more helpful people to you that will rent from you just because you helped a friend of theirs out on providing them with comfortable shelter. It's a give and take business. So try to keep an open mind for little things like that.

Who will look over your property if you invest in another State

Now this chapter is all about building positive cash flow and using management companies to manage your properties. Making money off properties by renting them out to individual is a great thing in my investment plan. If you are purchasing Real Estate through Tax Liens, you will not have to worry about paying a mortgage. For anything, the mortgage company will have to pay you to release the lien that you have on their property. Remember, Government and Federal liens override any mortgage collectors. Meaning, if the Grantor allow the property to go in a public auction for any reason, they have to pay the lien holder (which will be you) to redeem the property. The Grantor will pay you the lien amount plus interest because they do not want to lose their investment to a minor Tax Lien. They will deal with the property owner on their own time. That don't have anything to do with you. You're investing to receive interest on your money.

Most Grantors set up what they call an escrow account to prevent things like this from happen in the future. But if they don't! Then better for you, because you know your lien have a strong possibility of getting paid off. That's one good thing about being a lien holder. Tax Deeds are somewhat the same. You are buying the property free and clear so there will be no mortgages attach to the property. The sheriff or whomever is handling the sale will issue you a "As is" deed or what they call a "Sheriff deed" to the property.

Now foreclosures and buying from the seller is something totally different. You will have a mortgage to pay every month. Because foreclosures you are taking over the payments from the owner's down fall. And buying the property from the owner, nine times out of ten he/she have a mortgage to pay and they want someone else to pay it for them that's why they are selling or renting it out. Either way, they are somewhat bad investments to me, because you still have to pay a Grantor. Which can be a pain in the neck when you're working a regular 9 to 5 everyday.

When I perform seminar across the world to different cultures of people that would like to learn about this investment, I seem to be asked this question more than any, "Who will manage my property if I invest out of town?" I reply, "We all rented a apartment before right?" Most of the times everyone say yes. And then I ask, "Well who managed your apartment?" Then they say the Rental Office do. Well, the Rental Office is nothing more than a management company. They have management companies everywhere in the United States that will manage your properties for you for a reasonable fee. They will handle the following: maintains work, collecting rent, applications, finding tenants and checking up on the property for any damages that has been made. Some of them include other things in their contracts too. All you have to do is make sure your property taxes is paid and the insurance policy is updated. And some of the management companies even do that for you! They just send you a check in the mail for the remaining balance after their fees has been cleared.

The downside about this is that some companies won't manage your property if the neighborhood is infested with serious crimes. I had a property in Florida that the zoned management company literally said, "Are you crazy Mr. Jennings?" She said, "We don't go into that neighborhood!" That's why I said you have to do a full research on the property and its surroundings. You want to know as much as possible about the area and homes in that community. Investing in properties that the whole neighborhood needs improvements, may not be a good investment for you to sell or rent. No one wants to live in a community with a lot of abandoned houses. But! Sometimes that maybe just what you need, because they are the type of neighborhoods businesses like Hospitals and big Corporations take over.

Have you ever saw a neighborhood that was bad at first, but then changed over do to an community development? I'm going to use Baltimore for an example. Baltimore have a area that is very bad, but the Hospital (John Hopkins) buy homes from people in that area to build more sections for the Hospital. You never know! You may can play hard ball with that situation to get a great deal for your piece of trash. So don't always give up because the neighborhood is not so good. Just do your research first to see what the community developers have planned for that area.

Okay Javonte', what is Tax Deeds?

Okay, now we know that Tax Liens is when you are lending someone money to pay their taxes and you just receive a percentage from them unless that loan is not paid off when its redemption period is up. Which will lead to court arrangement for the sheriff to have a sale for the deed.

Now, Tax Deeds are more clear of a purchase then a lien. Some states will give the homeowners up to 5 years to pay their Taxes. And then the state will take full possession of their home and advertise it to be sold at a public auction. At that time, the bid will start from the back taxes.

The auctioneer will start the auction off by reading the description to the property. And then he/she will start the bid off with just the back taxes and it will go up only if others are bidding on it. If no one decides to bid on it, then you can purchase it for just the back taxes and fees. The highest bidder will receive a free a clear deed to the property. The only state I know that does this without giving the investor a free and clear deed is Texas.

Texas has something like both, Tax Liens and Deeds mixed in one. They use the deed format, but the owner has 6 months to redeem the property back from you with a 25% interest rate. That's sweet! But you don't actually own the property until the redemption period is up. And even then you have to pay the county to do the transferring of the deed.

Tax Liens and Deeds you are gambling by purchasing these properties "As is." But, would you rather buy a home for a couple of thousand, and only have to put a couple more thousand into it? Or, be over charged for a home that you could of brought the same way as the Grantor? Think about that for a moment.

Why don't Realtors tell people about this way to buy homes?

You have to understand that the Realtors are not your friends. They simply have to make money by selling homes to people that don't no better. The Realtor game is more like, "Who can we jerk as a dummy?" They are not out to help you! I know some of them may have nice personalities, but that's all! They are out to get the dummy whose going to spend the money.

Realtors receive a commission off every property they sell. If they don't sell, they don't get paid. With just that being said, can't you vision where they will tell you anything to get paid? Just put yourself in their shoes. Lets say you was a Realtor and you have to pay your bills in order to survive. Wouldn't you be on the grind to make money? Even if you did have to keep people from certain knowledge? Don't be honest with me, be honest with yourself.

Now, lets brush up on why they don't tell you about this type of investment. I am going to be straight forward with you. Most of them don't even know about Tax Liens. Maybe Deeds. But not Tax Liens. How can you tell people about something you never learned in school. They can't! Schools try not to teach them this type of investment. (I know because I have close friends that are Realtors). If everybody knew about these magnificent investments, they will be out of jobs, because you can't sell to people that know the same or more than you. However, sometime Realtors can be good help for information on Foreclosures, neighborhood developments, Tax laws, Home estimate cost, Real Estate forms, and much more.

You may want to consider building a good relationship with your Realtor in order for him/her to give you this type of information for free. I've learned to build good relationships with people I know I may need in my investment plans. And you should do the same if you would like to stand out from the other investors. Building friendship with Realtors to help your investment plan can bring great success. Don't let the high voice and body language fool you. They are human like you and I. They breath the same air as you and I. So don't be intimidated by their actions and body language.

Also keep in mind that you don't necessarily have to use a Realtor to buy a home. You can always go to the recorders office to find out who owns the property and simply approach them yourself. Don't be afraid to say, "I can do this myself," and mean it. Have any of you ever went to view a home with a realtor, did you notice that they always try to do what I call a "rush you." That means, they try not to let you examine the house fully. They show you everything fast and then want you to make a decision to purchase. Next time you go see a home tell them this, "I would like to examine the home by myself for an hour or two, to see if this is what I am really looking for."

Keep in mind that you are spending your money and you will have to deal with this home for a long period of time.

Ask some of your friends and family that faced the Foreclosure process, what was their reason for losing their home? You want to ask questions like this to prevent the mistakes they've mad. Now you have some people that are a little smarter and ahead then others. They pay off their mortgages ahead of time when they run into extra money. But for most people, they pay their mortgages as if their renting. They get extra money and they don't even look at the fact that they can hurry up and get the payments out the way before they lose their job or have some type of down fall that will lead to them losing their home. It just doesn't make sense to me! If you can become stress free, why not?

This sounds like a scam! Why should you believe me?

All I am going to say to you is that you have to do what? RESEARCH The next time you get on the computer, here's what I want you to do. I want you to think to yourself what city and state you will like to invest in and once you come up with an answer, just go to www.Google.com.

Now when you go to www.Google.com you will type in the city you wish to invest in and then type in "Tax Collectors" after it. Now all you have to do is call the Tax Collector's office and ask them for the next Tax Lien auction date? Oh, you will have to know if they offer deeds or liens too. They will provide you with the next auction date, what they require for you to participate in the auction, and everything else that you need to know in order to participate in the auction.

I have to laugh at this statement because it's true. These people can be real cranky at times. They act as if you are getting on their nerves from the start. Don't be rushed off the phone by these people. They get paid to answer any questions you have,

Once you've receive the information for the upcoming auction, then you want to get prepared for online auction bidding. If you asked enough question, they should have gave you their county auction website and it will give you an demo as if you was attend the auction. This is to practice for online bidding.

Now, to tell you the truth, I'm not going to beg you to do these things so you can become successful. As I said before, the people who want a better life will read and learn, others may never apply the knowledge. It's totally up to you rather or not you will use the knowledge that's giving to you. I can't invest for you. Only you can do that.

More investing! You can help people facing Foreclosure

Foreclosure investing is one of the worse ways to invest in Real Estate from my opinion. Unless you're a responsible person that is good at taking over someone else payments. When processing foreclosures, you want to be the first to get to them, because they can become difficult when they're at the end of the time line. The main key is getting to them before other investors step in the picture. Now, remember when I said you want to build a good relationship with the Realtors to keep you in the game? While Realtors will be able to get their hands on these properties way before anyone else will. The thing about foreclosure, is that you want to catch them at the beginning of the "Time Line."

The Time Line is when the owner is going through a period of how much time they have left before the Grantor take their home away from them. This change from state to state on how long the "Time Line" is.

You can find foreclosures in many different ways. The most common way is in the newspapers. In the back of each newspaper (in every state) they have what they call "Notice of sale," or "Legal Notice." In this notice they have the property's full description, Grantor conducting the sale, phone numbers, address to the Grantors, the current home owners name, the property address, when the last time the property was recorded, what county the property is located in, and much more valuable information. We will also give you an example of the "Legal Notice" in the back of the book. The Legal Notice will give you all the information you need to know in order to contact the property owner and the Grantor to investigate rather or not you will be interested in taking over the owner's payments.

Most of the time when people are facing foreclosure, they've either lost their job or the owner past away. Sometimes people just fall back on payments do to the misunderstand of their contract with the Grantors. Most contracts you have to go over with a lawyer to get a full understanding of the fine print these contracts are liable to have. Some contracts are written in big vocabulary words that most people don't understand, so they just sign without getting a full understanding of what they just singed. Some Grantors get people to agree to them raising the interest rate at anytime. That's why some people face foreclosure do to the misunderstanding of the contract.

When you approach someone that is facing foreclosure, most of the times they are very cranky, and they will not listen to you telling them the truth about them losing their home soon. For some reason, most homeowners think that they can negotiate with the Grantor for them to keep their homes for a little bit longer until they fine a job. LOL! These Grantors are not that nice of people. They don't understand that type of language. All they know is money! And if you don't have that, then when the time line is up, you're out. They don't see things like a ordinary person as you and I would. They work more like machines. Money machines that is!

To me, purchasing foreclosure is like taking over someone else dept. They pay a nice percents to live in the home for awhile and then you take over where they left off at.

You can ask for different terms and conditions that the current owner does not have in the previous contract. Foreclosure can be a great investment if you do it right. Right meaning, get to them first and keep good records on the property.

Communication is everything!

Communication is everything! When you are getting to know the foreclosure system, you will notice that you have to do a lot of communicating. You will see yourself playing hockey with the homeowners to the Grantor to paperwork and even the recorder's office. It can be a very stressful transaction. But just keep in mind that communication is everything. In most cases you will be dealing with the seller for the transaction of the deed. Once you've got in contact with the homeowner, and you've discuss the terms of how you will negotiate the deal on taking over the payments, then the only persons you have to convince of this matter is the Grantors.

Most of the time the Grantors will be in agreement of any terms that you and the homeowner has made at long as their signer is on the "Quit Claim" deed forms. The Grantors will transfer the deed over to you because they are not really concern about who pay them, their main concern is that the property is getting paid off. But, most Grantor will do a job history and credit check. The job history and credit check will determine rather or not you are qualified to take over the payments. Once you have cleared everything with the seller and the Grantor, you must then go to the recorders office to get your deed recorded. This may involve a very small fee of about ten to fifteen dollars. But this is the finishing touches of transferring the deed into your name.

Oh, one more thing, you also have to get property insurance. To do so, you have to contact a insurance company. Paying insurance on your property will give you coverage over your belongings just in case anything was to happen to your property. Property insurance also covers different objects in your home that may be valuable to you if ruined.

Ways to sell your properties online

There are plenty of ways to sell your property online. One of the best ways to do so is to hire a Realtor, because they know how to target buyers best. Realtors also know the requirements the states want to sell properties. This is not an easy process for someone that choose to do it themselves, but it can be done. The first thing you want to do is list your property with all the online websites that allows you to advertise real property. Listing your property with these websites will give you the advantage to have many different people see your home and call or email you about their interest in your property.

Like I've told you before, I very seldom sell properties so I don't know much about selling online, I would just say be careful for them websites that are not right. They ask for all your information then scam you in some way. But for the most part, a Realtor will fit perfect in selling property. Because they know what needs to be done.

Want to sell your property yourself?

Now me personally, I don't think you're wrong for wanting to sell your property yourself. However, there are requirements. In order to follow the rules and regulation by law, I would suggest for you to talk to an Realtor or an Title company for more advice. These rules varies from state to state. It can be a stressful transaction, so don't think for one second that its going to be a piece of cake (its only your birthday when you sell). The Realtor will have the forms you will need to complete the transaction. You can transfer the deed in many ways. When dealing with cash, and a ran down road home, you may want to "Quit Claim" your rights to the property. This is saying that you are transferring the property with no warranties and "As is." That way if there is something wrong with the property, you won't be held accountable for it.

The opposite is called a "General Warranty Deed". This is when you are giving the new property owner a warranty on the property. You are agreeing to being held accountable for anything that's wrong with the property and agreeing to fix the problem. The new owner may take you to court if you decide not to stick to your agreement. If you have any doubts that something may go wrong in the future (or however long the warranty is for) then this may not be a good deed to offer to the buyer.

The third Deed is call "Grant Deed." This is when the title has not been transferred previously and not any encumbrances, other than in the deed.

The last deed that I know of is called a "Special warranty Deed." It's less of a warranty because basically it's "as is."

Another way to draw attention to your home is to have open house. People seem to fill comfortable with open house sessions, because they can view the home and envision themselves living there without having someone showing them around, That's one of the best ways to draw buyers to your home.

Buying a property from the seller

One of the biggest secrets to entering the Millionaire lifestyle is negotiating! Negotiating in any field will get you ahead in life. Example, lets say you want a car that is priced at $41,000.00. The seller is saying they want $41,000.00, but in all actual reality that don't mean he or she won't take less. When someone is saying they want a certain price for something, what they really are saying is, "If someone is dumb enough to give me what I ask for then cool!" In their mind their thinking, "I'll take this number ($29,000.00) for it, but I'm going to put this ($41,000.00) number on it just in case they come short." And believe it or not, this same secret goes for almost everything that plays a part in life. Cars, homes, items that you get from the store, etc. You just have to have what I call "heart" to jump out there and start at a completely low price.

I'm going to use the above example for another example, Lets say the seller is asking for $41,000.00, and me knowing what I know as a millionaire. I'll start my price off at around $23,563.20. Now crazy people will think that's outrageous. Millionaires such as myself know that if the seller is selling, then it must be a reason. The reason can come from the following: The seller really need the money, the seller don't really want the product anymore, the seller has heath problems, the seller is leaving town, he or she may just want extra money for miscellaneous things, etc. There are thousands upon thousands of reasons the seller may be selling. Notice I use odd numbers too. I use odd numbers in negotiating because when you use odd number, that gives the seller a thought of that maybe all the money you have. When you talk even numbers, the seller have an good guess that you have more money to offer than what you're starting off with. And plus! Starting off with a low number will give you lots of room to negotiate. Remember this, you can always do the walk away fake. The walk away fake is something I do a lot and then they will call me back to see how we can work it out to make both of us happy. It works too! Sometimes you have to try things more than once and see how it works for you.

Okay after receiving my personal secrets, its time to get back on the topic which is Buying properties from the owner. Buying property from the owner is the same as the above. You have to throw low offers at the seller to get a response that works for you. A lot of times, (more than you may know) the seller is selling for a reason. One thing I learned in my couple of years of investing is that people don't sell homes just for the fun of it. Most of the times, they need the money more then you think they do. They may act as if they don't, but its a reason why they are selling. This can run as far as the state of Mississippi river, but it's a reason.

Me as the investor know not to try an agitate the seller, but try to ask questions that can't end with a simple yes or no. Ask questions that have to be explained and open up your mind with an following question. The seller will try their best to get every penny for their home, but most of the times, the seller is going off their emotion from the memories of their home. People seem to think of all the good and bad times they've had in their home and then price it at unreasonable prices do to them emotions on what they think their home is worth.

When homeowners are selling their homes themselves, be careful of violent acts when offering low numbers that may offend them. One thing homeowners don't understand is that as a Real Estate investor, you have to make good decisions for the future when purchasing property. When I do the numbers and they don't fit my investment plan, then I have to offer what works for me and only me. I can't give the seller what they ask for and then put myself at risk by paying more then what the property is worth.

Once I knew that Real Estate was something I would enjoy, I started making my own record sheets to keep everything about my properties together. And don't be afraid to use the walk away fake you've learned in the previous paragraphs. That works a lot when homeowners are being difficult negotiators on a deal.

Buying a property from a Realtor

As I said before, Realtor receive an commission off every sale they make. Now why should you pay someone for something you can do yourself? You shouldn't! But if you would like to go this wrought, then you may want to build a relationship with the Realtor that will show you your future home.

You wouldn't want to pick anyone that's just trying to make a sale. You want someone that can relate to how you think. If I was to pick a Realtor to show me homes, I would want a background check on that person experience. I want to know how many homes they sold in the past? How long have they been in the business? Why they chose to become a Realtor? Most importantly, how they communicate with others? And lots more. Think about it, this person have to be your back bone in business. They have to be able to negotiate with others in order to get you the best deal. Don't choose someone that have a nice personality but can't fight their way out of a plastic bag. Then they won't be able to give you the full potential of negotiating.

This is somewhere you have to live at for a long period of time, so just keep in mind that you never want to put your eggs in the wrong basket, no matter how many it is.

Definitions for Real Estate

Assessor—Someone that assesses property to determine the tax that will/ should be paid on it.

Grantor—a person or organization whom make grants.

Grantee—The receiver of a grant.

Zoning—pertaining to the division of an area into zones.

Recording Office—The state organization that's held accountable for keeping official records for each property that sits in the county/ city where the property is located.

Note Buyers—A person or organization whom buy Real Estate at a discount price.

Legal Notice—The announcement of sale by law pertaining to the foreclosure of someone's home.

Loan—The act of borrowing from someone or lending company.

Redemption—Redeeming.

Redeem—To buy back or recover.

Realtor—A Real Estate agent who is a member of the National Association of Realtors.

Appraiser—The person that judge the worth of your property.

Real Estate—Land and anything on it, including buildings, water, trees, etc.

Secession 2

Car Auctions

Car Auctions

Car auctions is a very exciting investment. Not just because you will want every car for yourself, but you can make huge profits from this very simple investment. Car auctions is conducted by what they call auctioneers, who seem to talk very fast when presenting the bids. The auctions is held when an owner of a car doesn't pay the impound the fees to release their car to them. It can also be held for cars that's been seized from the owner for what ever reason.

Many times the reason for the auction is because no one came to pickup their car. I will teach you how to make huge profits from this very secretive investment. Many people keep it a secret because they may not want competition, may not want anyone to know how they're becoming rich very fast, it could be because they want this to be for the people that already know about it. However, despite the reasons why they won't tell you, because when reading this section of the book, you will have everything you need to be an successful investor.

How to get started?

Okay the first thing you want to do to be a successful investor is to make up a chart that will help you organize your path to investing. You will see an example in the back of the book to help you decide what you choose to make for your "Investment Plan" chart. After making your chart, then you want to look in the phone book to find out where all the Car Auctions is been held at. Most of the time, for public auctions, you will find them right at the Car impound lot.

Once you've found out where you will be attending for the auction, then you want to find out the time scheduled to be there. When speaking to the receptionist, always ask as many questions as possible. Ask them how many people usually attend their auctions, ask them how many days can you keep the car you bid on in their lot without paying for storage space? These will be useful questions to ask because this will give you strategies on how you will become a successful investor.

Getting started is the easy part! The question you should be asking yourselves is this: What am I going to do with all these cars? Notice I used, "all of these cars?" I said that because once you go to your first auction and you see the way the cars get brought for pennies on the dollar, you will want to go to one every time they come around. I've been in this business for quite some time now, and I always see cars go for under $200.00, and these is good workable cars we're talking about.

My first time going to an auction I pulled out a Caprice with 22 inch rims for less then $300.00, NO EXAGGERATING The car was in very good condition and had a Cd player along with leather seats. Now I'm not saying these cars don't need a little attention because some of them do. For the most part all of them do! But let me ask you this, would you rather purchase a car from a dealer that's doing the same thing I'm teaching you about for double the price you could of brought it for? If so, then this book may not be for you. This is to teach the people that don't like having to make a payment every month. For the people that's tired of being taken advantage of.

Me personally, I build good relationships with my components. I like to know how they sell cars on their spare time, what type of profits they want to receive on each car they purchase. And much more! I like to know my market very well so that I can do what will make me a better investor then them.

How do you know if these cars work?

One thing about attending an auction, is that you may not know the valid condition of the vehicle into you get an diagnose test on it. But, they do have numbers for what the cars is there for. Say if the car's been taken from someone by the police, then they will have a certain number for that particular reason. They also have cars that's been stolen, crash, abandon and from parking tickets. Each one will have their own number written on them for the reasons they are there. Some auctions won't tell you what the codes mean if you don't ask, but for some auctions, you may have the securities help you out on what codes mean what for a small fee. That is not fair! If they tell you to give them money and they'll tell you what the codes mean, you tell them to give you the numbers for free or else you'll report it to there boss. They are not allow to take advantage of you like that.

My first time going to a car auction, these two ladies (securities) got over on me like that. I watched them make around $70.00 by telling bidders the codes. They went around to tell investors that they knew the codes and if they give them a couple of dollars they will give them the codes. Bidders that was new to the process gave in and they made ten dollars each from the bidders. They can lose there jobs by doing such thing. They get paid from pay checks not by telling people what they should already be telling them. So just watch out for that.

When you get into a regular routine, you will become better each time. You will come up with strategies that will be useful to you as a successful bidder. One thing I do recommend you to do is make sure you bring a mechanic with you to do research on the cars. Most of the time, they will be willing to do this for a very very low fee if you let them work on the car. They like to have consistence business. So anytime they can setup a good business partnership that will keep coming to them, it's a strong possibility they will do so. I will explain to you how I started off in the next few chapters. And always know that just because a car works at that time, don't necessarily mean it's a good buy. Sometimes sellers may know exactly what the car needs to run for a while to sell it to you and get away with it. But that's when you are dealing with a seller instead of a auction. At auctions the cars may have been sitting for a while so you may have to get a tune-up before driving. A lot of time, the battery may be dead too, so a lot of people won't bid on it, which makes it a good deal for you because if you don't have any competition then you can walk away with a good buy for less then you would of spent at the dealership.

What's the best way to advertise?

The best way to sell your cars would be to have costumer already lined up to purchase the car you went to the auction for. But of course that wouldn't be for someone that just started out selling cars. The best way I would recommend for you to sell cars just starting off is to list them in the newspapers, Craigslist, Ksl, and other resources that allow you to advertise cars.

When I first started off, I had a good relationship with a gas station owner and we talked it over for me to sell cars on his property. He agreed to receive 20% off each car I sold. Now as business picked up, he canceled our deal to use my strategy against me. He started doing what I had told him I was doing. But the point I'm trying to get across is that I knew by him having a lot of costumers coming there for his product, they was going to be curious about my product as well. I keep a good quality of cars and never have to worry about people coming back to complain because my mechanic always do his job correct. Another way I made money was putting my cars in shopping centers with high traffic. They seem to be the best places to advertise cars at because people is always around looking for opportunities for deals. You know, like places that have laundromat, markets, and other places that many people go for different reasons. Now I'm not telling you to do the same thing as I did, because some times you can get a fine for advertising in the wrong places. But you want to put your cars somewhere you can sell quick. Like another thing I did and still do is put cars on busy streets. That's where most of my profits came from.

I put vehicles on busy streets with shoe polish on the front window to let people know I'm selling, and most of the time I sell within two weeks of it being there. I receive huge profits and clientele from this strategy. Even though I'm in partnership with a dealer now, I still look for ways to make money outside of that just in case things don't work out as we agreed. The plan is to have things establish so that if you ever pass away, you can have a structured foundation to leave to your love ones. And the only way to do so is to build it up to a strong organization for them to follow when you leave.

I have friends that love using these strategies and make good money doing it. But I always tell them to look at the bigger dream. Look at owning your own dealership, because selling them on the streets and at shopping centers is good because you're making profits, but do you want to do that forever? That cost a lot of stress on me personally. I was doing to much running around to move them, check on the condition of it, showing them to people that changed their minds on rather or not they was going to buy it, etc. I had this one guy had me believing that he had the money with him to buy it, and then after the joyride to clarified that the car worked great, he told me that he was going to meet me the next day to purchase it. I had drove about 4 ½ miles to show him this vehicle, and then he told me to meet him the next day. I was very angry!

It was easier for me to open up the dealership to keep everything I own in one spot. That way if someone want to trade, buy, or sell, I can help them right here on the spot on what ever services they need. So to answer your question, the best way to advertise is to just do it the right way and get your dealers license. And believe it or not, it's not that hard to do. I will tell you how I became partners with a dealer in the next chapter.

How I became a dealer

I became a Dealer by talking with a dealer almost every week. It got to the point I knew his situation on what type of help he was looking for. So as we got to know each other a little better, he came out and asked me was I interested in going in Business together. He said, "you come around here a little to much to not be looking for a partner." He asked me about my financial status and how many cars I had.

The problem was he was trying to get a bigger lot and he had no one to take on the challenge with him. To me his lot was already a nice size for the cars that he had advertised, but what I didn't know is that he had another smaller lot on the other side of town that was doing good numbers.

So as we talked more about the goals that he was trying to meet, I knew this would be the guy I invest my money in because of his intelligence for the business as a whole. For me, I know with my criminal background I may not be able to become the second owner, so we just made a plan for me to work for him under state laws, pay the lot fees, and still receive benefits as if I was the second owner. It works out perfect for me because knowing that I may never get a chance to own my own dealership, I still have inns on partnership.

To tell you the truth, I'm still in training of the whole dealer thing. I'm use to the street selling. And until this day I still have cars that I sell on the busy streets. But it's going very well for my first 4 months in the business.

Now I let him know that I would be mentioning our business in this book, and he told me that it was okay. However, I would rather keep our business off of paper to keep a good relationship between us. So to brake down how we do business would be disrespect in my eyes towards him. So the above is just the general idea of how I became a dealer. Now if I was to ever get my own Dealers Licenses through the state. Then I would write my second book on how I profit in this business. But as a partner, I think that should remain confidential.

What's my advice

My advice to anyone that wants to invest in their own future would be to study everything I say from the beginning to the end of this book. Think about the possibilities of how long you will have a job. Think about how many times the economy will claim to go down. You see, with these secrets you will never take in the words of a recession. That don't even exist to a person like me because I know in this world you have to be the one that apply the knowledge to be successful.

I'm probably the only investor that will give you all the knowledge to be successful. Most investors will tell you a little, and with that little that they do tell you, they will sugarcoat most of their knowledge. Or, try to make things seem harder then what they really are to change your mind about investing.

I watch many people get talked out of their dreams because they listened to other people's negative thoughts or experiences. Don't listen to people that have negative things to say about your dreams. When people talk bad about something that you want to do, it's usually for many different reason than the ones they are telling you. It could be because they don't have the money to do it, they can be jealous (friends and family included), they may not want you to reach past their level, they may want to just stir you wrong, or they may have not been educated on what you want to do but act as if they are. It can be numerous of reasons that someone may talk bad about your dreams, but you have to be the one that say, "I'm going to make this person a liar."

Many people are afraid to take risk, but the only way to grow rich is to take risk. They rather buy merchandise from people that's doing the same thing they can do. That's why I tell you the secrets of my own even though I'm a secretive person. I know many people will never read or may never apply the knowledge. Some will read but still choose to spend their money with me or another dealer. That's great! But think of the payments that you're going to have to make every month. I don't mine using the money to invest in another car or two, but you can't say I didn't warn you. I just like to see everybody profit in life not just friends and family.

And some family won't listen. Oh well! They seem to get mad and hate on me because I'm wealthy, but they don't want to listen to become as me. They rather build hate in there minds then follow the road I choose. As the reader you may know actually what I'm talking about with your own families, but you have to keep moving to the top and don't stress about their faults.

How many cars can you sell without paying taxes

You can only sell a certain amount of cars in your state without paying taxes or being required to get your Dealers licenses. The number of how many cars you can sell change from state to state. Best way to find out how many cars you can sell is to contact your local DMV and they will provide that to you along with other valuable information.

Where can you get used parts from

You can get used car parts from many different places. One useful place to get any type of car part is at a car Junk Yard. They will have almost any type of car you need to take parts off of. You can even use parts from other cars to fix your car up to how you would like it to look. I took a old Crown Victoria and changed it into what looks like a Crown Victoria and Impala in one.

Some times you may hear this Junk Yard go by the name of "Pick and Pull." If you see something that have this name or something similar, then you know you're in the right place. Pick and Pulls are located on main highways most of the time. But you can easily find where your closes Pick and Pull is at by going on the internet or using the phone book to look them up.

You can also go on the internet to some of the websites that was mentioned like Craigslist and Ksl, or any other websites that allow people to sell their cars. Look for people that's selling parts only. This can be an excellent way to purchase parts because you can make everything negotiable.

When I go to the auction, I look for abandoned cars to make projects out of. I use these cars to stripe whatever good parts they have on them and then I sell the reminder parts that I don't need. Being as though I purchase them for dirt cheap, I try to get what I need and then sell it for the same price I purchase it for. When you sell it, you may want to tell the person what's been taken off it for good relationships in the future. You want to make money, but you don't want people looking for you because you did them wrong by selling them a bad car. But! You don't have to tell them how much you brought it for. The good thing about the auction is that you can buy cars that's in excellent body condition. You can use this to your advantage because that's what most body shops are looking for in a car. When they have the advantage to add parts and deduct parts from under the hood, that's what makes them happy about their jobs. The shop that I go to like experiment on their personal cars. They take cars and turn them into race cars. It's awesome!

It may be more places to purchase used car parts from that I don't know of. Since I've been in this business, they have been my main sources for used car parts. Of course you can purchase brand new parts too. You can go to Pep Boys or Auto Zone to order whatever parts you need. They will also put it in too if you pay them to do it. But then you will be paying for the parts and the labor work. So just take that in consideration. Also take in consideration that if you're buying new parts for a used car, you want to be sure that you're going to have it for a while.

I never put too much money into an auction car because my objective is to sell and not to keep for my own pleasure. As an investor, you never want to put more money into something that will not make its money back. Cars are one of those investments that loses value. The moment you pull off the lot in that new car you just brought, the value of the car goes down. A little different then Real Estate.

Who can you get to fix your cars

There are many mechanics that can fix your cars. If you are an investor that will make a regular routine of investing, then you may want to do your homework on different mechanics to get a good deal and to build that business relationship for on going business.

Getting anyone that claim to be a mechanic to fix your cars may be a big mistake! You are getting prepared to sell this same car to someone else that may not take your mistake so lightly. You want someone that have a shop and known for doing great work. What is great work? Great work is when you don't have to bring the car back a week later for the same problem. Someone that will do something extra on the car for no cost to build trust and reputation for future references.

If you read closely, notice I said for the same problem. I said this because if you get anyone to do the work on your car, they may take other parts off your car so that you can come back next week to get that fix too. Some mechanics do that to have a job later on down the line. It may be funny but it's true. Some mechanics are so good at what they do, you will never know that something else was done to your vehicle into it start acting up.

Another thing I do is watch them as they fix my car. They don't like that because most of the time they get paid by the time they spend fixing your vehicle. I observe mechanics sit around and talk for hours without laying one finger on people's cars, but they charge them for the time that their car been in the shop. They are scanless people at times if you study how they do business. But being on top of them will give you the advantage from them taking advantage of you.

Just know who you are doing business with before you decide to have them apart of your organization, because that will fall back on you if something was to go wrong with the vehicles you're selling. And trust me, you don't want to get sued for something that could have been avoided by doing research on your mechanic.

Walking away happy

You know when you've just did a good deal, because you will walk away happy and confidence in yourself to do it again. If you fill good about yourself that means you are sure and happy about the following: The car will run for a while, the price worked for you and the buyer, you made the profit you was wishing you'd make on the deal, the parts are not bad or stolen on the vehicle, the title and everything else is legit, and knowing you are heading back to the auction to buy another car to do the same thing you've just done.

This is an awesome filling, but remember that you have to check with your state to see how many times you can do this without paying taxes or been required to have your Dealers licenses. This can and more than lightly will change from state to state.

Definitions for Car auctions

Car—Automobile that runs on a street as a vehicle.

Scrap—Small portions of the vehicle or sold as a whole.

Junk Yard—A huge yard for the collection, storage, and resale of junk.

Abandon—To give up. To leave completely and finally.

Used—Owned or previously used; second hand.

Dealership—a distributor who has authorization to sell.

Auctioneer-a person who conduct sales by auctions.

Impound—to seize and retain in custody of the law for evident.

Secession 3

Storage Auctions

Storage Auctions?

Storage Auctions get's me jacked out my mind! They are so exciting to attend and you never know what you're going to get. Way before the television show about storage auctions start coming on, my father use to always tell me about this time him and his Wife went to one. He said he wasn't there to bid on anything, but he saw the people waiting around and was curious of why they was standing there. As he hung around and asked questions about what was going on, he said he found out a lot of information about what was about to happen. He said, "when those doors pop Javonte', I was shock that things like storage auctions even exist." From the energy that he gave off, I knew this would be a very interesting investment.

My family was a victim of this investment at an early age of development. My mother had put some things of ours in storage when I was a kid. I said that this is a world of control, offense and defense. Well now tables have turned and now I'm on the investor side of life. Do you see what I was talking about when I said the Government sets up a system for Rich or Poor? This is a good example for that speech. Either you pay your bills or the storage company gets authorization from the higher power to sell your property.

Bidding Methods

Unlike taxes liens, this investment have two different bidding methods that I know of. They have what we call silent bidding, that's when you are not actually bidding on the unit right then and there, you are looking at the unit and then you write your bid on the form that they give you. After the looking part is finish, then the auctioneer will take everyone's form and call out the winner. But I also had this done another way too. In one city I was in, they had these forms that had all the units and the numbers to them. They had everyone look at the units, write their bids down on the paper to past in, and then they call the winner of each unit out at the end of the auction. We had to look at all the units first before they told us who the winner was. That was a little weird because I had never done it that way before. But almost all the investments I teach in this book will change from city to city, state to state, from county to county. Every storage have their own rules.

I don't know of any other methods that they use because I don't travel the world for this investment. I'm just familiar with my county storage auctions. I will only know the rules for my location for how ever long I'm there.

What can this investment do for you

This investment has done more for me than I done for myself. I have got the things I needed plus more. Just think about the things that you need in your home such as: Couches, tables, bedroom sets, mirrors, miscellaneous things that you will usually have around your home and much more. This is one of those investment that you'll never know what you're going to find in the units. Think of it as if you was facing this crisis, what type of things would you put in storage? Okay know come back to reality and picture how many people are facing losing their units and how many items you can pick up on for pennies on the dollar.

Don't fill bad

A lot of people that I introduce to these investment seem to get upset with themselves because they think that they are taking advantage of other people. Well good news for you if this is the way you fill. Before the auction date comes up, the owner has a chance to either pay the bill or get his or her stuff out of the unit. They are giving a chance to do this without any extra fees. Maybe if they're late on the rent, but not if they would like to remove the property from the unit. So as an investor you are taking over the stuff that they left there to be sold. Most of the time, the people just don't have the money or space to put all their items, that's why they are leaving it to be sold.

The only reason the storage company is having the auction is to clear the space for availability for someone else that need to place there belongings there for a fee. The company really don't profit much from doing this. They are doing it because they have nowhere else to put the property. They only make money when someone pay there bill for that month. So when they auction someone items off they are just getting back what was owed. Sometimes they profit even more if the bidders run the bid up. But that depends on what's in the unit.

How much time do you have to clear the unit

Depending on the storage company and their policy, you will have a certain amount of time to clear the unit out before you have to pay for a lease or money for the extra time that it sits in there. Most auctions will include this time-frame in the rules before they actually start the bid on the units. Majority of the time, you have to the next day to clear the unit out. But it can be different for that company so just ask questions if you're not 100% sure of the answer.

They are not your friends

Okay so bidders are waiting until the auction start and they're talking to anyone in site. Remember this is your competition. They are on the other side of the fence, but there trying to play buddy so if you are bidding against them on a unit, you can give in because you was talking to them before the bidding started. Some people try to be slick to benefit themselves. But this is not always true.

Some people are looking to see what you're interesting in. They have no intentions on trying to get you to give in to them. You never know what you can swap out with other trash-men. They may be looking for an certain object that you have already or about to get. You may be a collector looking for specific items and they may know the right people to plug you in with.

All I'm saying is never have a close mind on business, try to keep an open mind on how you can help each other. Remember these secrets stay among the ones that know, and there are not many people that know about taking over other people's trash. So you may want to keep some of these people in your corner for long term vision.

Think about this for a minute, if you are an investor looking for a specific object and you know that it's hard to come pass, who will you call? You may run into that one friend that you met at the auction that can get his hands on it if he already don't have it. You don't have to be involved with a lot of friends, just one or two that have friends that invest so that you don't have to be the one to pick their brains.

Do you see the vision that I'm putting out their for you to cast. Its a million dollar investment if you get plugged in with the right people. Just communicate and always keep your eyes out for old items that may be a collectable to others.

Knowing the value of your product

Knowing the value of your product is one of the most stressful things if you are not an expert in getting out and finding the buyers you need to purchase your items. Let me tell you why. When you are receiving items that you're selling, you want to know how much you can get for your merchandise, but any Joe Blow can tell you it's worth one thing, and someone else can tell you something completely different. But the only person that you should be interested in knowing what they will pay for it is your buyers.

Dealing directly with a buyer you're going to have to negotiate the difference between what he/she will pay and what's the value of the merchandise. Buyers such as Pawn Shops will not be open to pay what you're asking for if they don't see a huge profit on their end. Pawn Shops are very tight on their budgets. But if you go somewhere were that business do nothing but deal with the item that you're bring to them, then it will make a big difference. Because that's what they are looking for so it will be easier for them to determine the value and offer you what they believe will be a good deal.

When you hear the numbers, don't be so quick to agree even if it is more than what you paid for the unit. Always try to get more out of it then what they offer you. Always keep in mind what I said about how the buyers and sellers is actually willing to pay more (or take less) then the first offer. They just want to see what you're going to say to that one first.

Secession 4

The Millionaire
dress code

The Millionaire Dress-code

The Millionaire dress code means more than just dressing up to impress others. This is the way the world is divide into two different worlds. For some people this means nothing, for others, this is the way they make the most money.

When you are dress nice, it gives other people a different respect for you. Lets say you are going to show someone a car and you have on a business suite, tie and handkerchief, colon, hair cut, finger nails trimmed, and last but not lease nice shoes to top it off. Don't you think your buyer are going to think you are there for business and business only? Its how real people that's out for profits dress. Now I'm not saying that you have to dress like this to make money because then that would be a lie. But if you would like to create a unique business future for yourself then you should apply this technique.

And think of it as if you was in the other person's shoes, would you rather spend your money with someone that's dress like they're professional, or someone that look like they're trying to scam you in someway? For example, if I came to you nails long and dirty, hair looking anyway, dress in t-shirt and jeans, with no smell, and beat down shoes. Would you feel comfortable giving me your money for whatever reason?

Now I'm not trying to turn you into models or anything, but you do want to impress your buyers, rather it's in Real Estate or selling a Car. With purchasing tax liens you don't have to do this into you are ready to present the home to a buyer. Because tax liens is done from a home-base business respective.

How to purchase cloths for cheap

If you was to ever met me in person, you would think that I'm some type of guy that go shopping every week or something. I learned as a child to save my money and to spend less on the things that really don't mean much in life. As a child I would always go to the Thrift Store to buy my cloths. I made good use of the little bit of money that I did get for allowance. You may think of it as if you are putting on someone's trash, well that is what this book is about so you can look at it like that. But let me tell you a secret, some of the world's most known Millionaires did the same at one point of time in there lives.

You will be amaze on some of the stuff you are going to find in the Thrift Store for pennies on the dollar that will cost you a couple of hundred in the original stores. I have so many shirts and suites that would of cost me as far as a couple of thousand or more. I buy nice things that will last for years and then I pass it down to new investors that come into our team. You have to apply this technique! See what's out there for you that you can pick up on for cheap and then have people think you're richer than what you really are. But if you apply this book into your life than you wouldn't be putting on a fake for them, you will really be rich.

The key to success is to make your mind strong for anything that may come your way. You want to be mentally, and emotionally, strong for your opponents and buyers. Looking up to part will help you build your confidence up. Watch and see! You're going to fill good because you look good. And believe it or not, it works.

Being court off guard

Using these strategy will create great wealth faster than you may know right now. When people see you dress nice and ready to use your mouth for negotiating a lot, then that's the person you're going to be known for when they see you again. The last thing you want to do is make a mistake and show them another person that you didn't attend to show them. So what I suggest you to do is set up some type of schedule for yourself. Pick out what days you will go out and do deals and what days will be your rest or family day. This will give the people around you an idea of what type of person you are. If they see you using this method, then they know that you are a very responsible person for your actions.

It also gives you balance in your everyday life. Being as though you will be use to a schedule, you will start using this to your advantage when you have other things to do on them days. I think you'll get the hang of it when it starts drawing people to you that will be helpful in your everyday life outside of Real Estate, Car Auctions, and Storage Auctions. With Car Auctions, you shouldn't really be dress up because most of the time you will be getting dirty from checking the cars out. Unless you build a team to do that for you.

And to tell you the truth, this is a very small country. You never know when you're going to see someone that you done business with before. Even if you're in another state. You will be surprised how many people I saw in different states that I done business with before. And I'm only 23 years of age and I like to travel, but I seem to always see someone that I know or done business with before. That's why I said you don't want to sell someone a messed-up car and think you're going to get away with it because what ever you do in the dark, comes out in the light.

Combinations

When you have nice cloths, cars, and houses to match your persona, people seem to look at you different. What they see is persistence and eager to succeed in life. They may just want to follow your lead just because they see that in your character. That's what you need when entering the road to success. You need others to rely on. You never know what may happen later on down the line; for example, like when you need some extra money to foreclosure on that home. You may need someone to drive a car back from the auction for you if you are not able to do it. The point I'm trying to get across is that you're going to need someone sometimes. So if you want to be successful, then you may want to start building them relationships now. And your dress code have more to do with this then you may think.

Walk to Walk

As I was coming up as a child I used a lot of profanity. I always had a small vocabulary but I knew how to use it to get by. When I started to get out in the real world and notice that everyone communicate in different ways, I knew it was time for me too step my communication skills up. Before I wrote this book I had just got started in a telecommunication company that is endorse by Donald J. Trump. And in this business, you have to hold presentations to build your team. Right then and there I knew that I had to learn a different way to communicate with people, because my old ways wasn't working for me anymore with the new lifestyle I was entering.

So do you want me to be completely honest with you on how I learned how to do this? I learn from watching movies. I watch different business and comedy movies to learn a mix personality. This old fashion method taught me how to make certain jokes to ease people up from getting angry. I learned how to shake people hands and look them directly in the eyes as I speak to them. It taught me how to be organized at all times so I wouldn't make myself look like a fool. Every time I look at a movie, I try to get something out of it other than what the original message is.

This can teach you to become a people's person and prepare you for different personalities. Just try it out when you get a chance. Use something that you've saw on a movie or from studying actual life situations. You will develop good communication skills if you strategist how to use them when the time presents itself.

I also went to the library to learn how to speak different languages other then English. They have books and CD's you can either take home or study there. That's why I always tell my friends, "you don't have to go to college to be a smart person, just use what God has giving you for free." Many things may cost money, but for me education is one thing that's always going to be free. You just have to be the one to seek and use it.

Writer Thoughts

You may be thinking to yourselves, why was this book so short but exciting? Well, this book was written to catch the attention of the youth and prisoners, because they're the ones that need it for their future dreams.

Think of it as if you was in my shoes and was looking forward to changing the world slowly be surely, who attention would you grab? Attract the children and prisoners, because that's the next generation that's being controlled by the Government and Presidents commands.

Hear you have people that's well over 70 years of age that never heard of a Tax Lien or Deed. Some people never knew you could purchase cars from the auction for less than what the Dealers are selling for. That's one of the main reason this book was written. To stop the miss-education of the children. So they can have nice things without having to be foreclosed on, or having to make a payment through car notes.

Many people never look at the facts in life. They setup this offense side of life for a reason. This is not illegal or cruel. This is something that our leaders of this country created for the people that want to be rich. They don't look at it as if you're taking advantage. So why should you?

Offense is a different side of the field. Most of us that are not in Secret Society are use to playing defense in life, that's why we are so close minded about playing offense. I'm not a cruel person, but I'm not a fool either! I am here on earth to learn, live, and benefit in anyway I can. But self-conscious tell you that you're wrong, because we was taught not to greed. Well I have bad news for you who think this is true, We was lied to!! You better greed if you don't want to be poor.

You have to pay for food, shelter, cloths, taxes on every dollar you spend or make, gas, transportation, and millions of other things that the spiritual God can't help you with (until he come back). So my advice to you would be to help yourselves and your family

I said help family because if you ever fall off the top, you can always go back to someone you helped get to there position. If you go through life not helping others get to were you are then you can cancel the plans on someone helping you in the future if things ever come down for you. Helping others is one of my specialties! I love to see the smile that it brings to other people face when they use something that they didn't know about before I approached them.

Legal Notice Sample

The following property will be sold to the highest bidder at a public auction at the time of sale at the south entrance of the Cedar City Hall of Justice, 40 N. 100 E., Cedar City, Utah, on June 19, 2010 at 11:00 a.m, to foreclosure a Trust Deed recorded November 23, 2008 as Entry No. 6666666, executed by PICK ON THE WEAK, as Trustor, in favor of Mortgage Electronic Registration System, Inc. as nominee for MILA, Inc. and its successors and assigns, covering real property in iron County. (Tax/ Parcel No.9-3475-0002-0000 (acct # 0996732)) purportedly, but not guaranteed to be located at 444 N. Jennings Rd. Cedars City UT 84720, together with, and subject to, any applicable improvements, fixtures, easements, appurtenances, taxes, assessment, conditions, covenants, restrictions, reservations or enforceable rights and obligations, and described as follows:

All of lot, PENNIES THEY PAY, PHASE 1, according to the official plat thereof on file in the office of the Iron County Recorder.

The current beneficiary of the Trust Deed is U.S. Bank National Association. As Trustee for the Specialty Underwriting and Residential Finance Trust Mortgage Loan Asset-Backed Certificates Series 2006-AB2 and as of the date the Notice of Default recorded, the property was owned by PICK ON THE WEAK according to the record. The successful bidder must tender a $5,000 non-refundable deposit at the sale, in the form of a cashier's/ official bank check payable to the Trustee, and deliver the balance in certified funds to the Trustee's office within 24 hours of the sale;otherwise, the Trustee reserves the right to sell the property to the next highest bidder, retain the deposit, and hold the defaulting bidder liable for any additional damages. The sale is without any warranty, including title, possession and encumbrance, and is voidable by the Trustee, without any liability, for any circumstance unknown to the Trustee affecting the validity of sale. If the Trustee voids the sale, the successful bidder's sole remedy is return of any funds tendered to the Trustee. THIS IS AN ATTEMPT TO COLLECT A DEBT, AND ANY INFORMATION OBTAINED MAY BE USED FOR THAT PURPOSE.

Dated June 2, 2010

/s/

Get Overs—Successor Trustee

6996 Take Advantage of the poor to stay rich St., S.L.C., UT 84109

(801) 666-7412—8:00 a.m-5:00 p.m

Attorney Reference No. 4126087478

Home Inspection Sheet

Property address: _____

Inspection Date: _____

<u>Inspection Item</u>

<u>Excellent Condition</u>   <u>Average Condition</u>   <u>Poor Condition</u>

Estimate Cost

Neighbors home : ( ) ( ) ( ) $.
Gutters : ( ) ( ) ( ) $.
Lawn: ( ) ( ) ( ) $.
Roof: ( ) ( ) ( ) $.
Landscaping: ( ) ( ) ( ) $.
Driveway: ( ) ( ) ( ) $.
Walk and Steps: ( ) ( ) ( ) $.
Fence: ( ) ( ) ( ) $.
Mail Box: ( ) ( ) ( ) $.
Porch and Decks: ( ) ( ) ( ) $.
Outside Electrical Fixture: ( ) ( ) ( ) $.
Windows and Screens: ( ) ( ) ( ) $.
Outside Storage: ( ) ( ) ( ) $.
Shutters: ( ) ( ) ( ) $.
Septic System: ( ) ( ) ( ) $.
Drainage: ( ) ( ) ( ) $.
Foundation: ( ) ( ) ( ) $.
Walls: ( ) ( ) ( ) $.
Other: ( ) ( ) ( ) $.
Other: ( ) ( ) ( ) $.

General Walk Through

Door Bell: ( ) ( ) ( ) $.
Security System: ( ) ( ) ( ) $.
Smoke Detectors: ( ) ( ) ( ) $.
Intercom: ( ) ( ) ( ) $.
Heat System: ( ) ( ) ( ) $.
Cooling System: ( ) ( ) ( ) $.
Sump Pump: ( ) ( ) ( ) $.
General Cleanliness and odor: ( ) ( ) ( ) $.
Water Heater: ( ) ( ) ( ) $.
Water softener/ Filter System: ( ) ( ) ( ) $.
Washer/ Dryer Connection: ( ) ( ) ( ) $.
Other: ( ) ( ) ( ) $.

Living Room

Floor Covering: ( ) ( ) ( ) $.

Fireplace: ( ) ( ) ( ) $.

Door and Locks: ( ) ( ) ( ) $.

Closet: ( ) ( ) ( ) $.

Window Treatment: ( ) ( ) ( ) $.

Window Screen: ( ) ( ) ( ) $.

Light Fixtures: ( ) ( ) ( ) $.

Walls and Ceilings: ( ) ( ) ( ) $.

Other: ( ) ( ) ( ) $.

Other: ( ) ( ) ( ) $.

Dining Room

Floor Covering: ( ) ( ) ( ) $.
Fireplace: ( ) ( ) ( ) $.
Door and Locks: ( ) ( ) ( ) $.
Closet: ( ) ( ) ( ) $.
Window Treatment: ( ) ( ) ( ) $.
Window Screen: ( ) ( ) ( ) $.
Light Fixtures: ( ) ( ) ( ) $.
Walls and Ceilings: ( ) ( ) ( ) $.
Other: ( ) ( ) ( ) $.
Other: ( ) ( ) ( ) $.

Den

Door and Locks: ( ) ( ) ( ) $.
Floor Covering: ( ) ( ) ( ) $.
Light Fixtures: ( ) ( ) ( ) $.
Windows: ( ) ( ) ( ) $.
Walls and ceilings: ( ) ( ) ( ) $.
Fireplace: ( ) ( ) ( ) $.
Other: ( ) ( ) ( ) $.
Other: ( ) ( ) ( ) $.

Kitchen

Doors and Locks: ( ) ( ) ( ) $.
Floors covering: ( ) ( ) ( ) $.
Light Fixtures: ( ) ( ) ( ) $.
Walls and ceiling: ( ) ( ) ( ) $.
Windows: ( ) ( ) ( ) $.
Other: ( ) ( ) ( ) $.
Other: ( ) ( ) ( ) $.

Master Bedroom

Doors and Locks: ( ) ( ) ( ) $.
Floors covering: ( ) ( ) ( ) $.
Light Fixture: ( ) ( ) ( ) $.
Walls and ceiling: ( ) ( ) ( ) $.
Windows: ( ) ( ) ( ) $.
Closets: ( ) ( ) ( ) $.
Other: ( ) ( ) ( ) $.
Other: ( ) ( ) ( ) $.

Bedroom 1

Doors and Locks: ( ) ( ) ( ) $.
Floor covering: ( ) ( ) ( ) $.
Light Fixtures: ( ) ( ) ( ) $.
Walls and ceilings: ( ) ( ) ( ) $.
Windows: ( ) ( ) ( ) $.
Closets: ( ) ( ) ( ) $.
Other: ( ) ( ) ( ) $.
Other: ( ) ( ) ( ) $.

Bedroom 2

Doors and Locks: ( ) ( ) ( ) $.
Floor covering: ( ) ( ) ( ) $.
Light Fixtures: ( ) ( ) ( ) $.
Walls and ceilings: ( ) ( ) ( ) $.
Windows: ( ) ( ) ( ) $.
Closets: ( ) ( ) ( ) $.
Other: ( ) ( ) ( ) $.
Other: ( ) ( ) ( ) $.

Bedroom 3

Doors and Locks: ( ) ( ) ( ) $.
Floor covering: ( ) ( ) ( ) $.
Light Fixtures: ( ) ( ) ( ) $.
Walls and ceilings: ( ) ( ) ( ) $.
Windows: ( ) ( ) ( ) $.
Closets: ( ) ( ) ( ) $.
Other: ( ) ( ) ( ) $.
Other: ( ) ( ) ( ) $.

Bedroom 4

Doors and Locks: ( ) ( ) ( ) $.
Floor covering: ( ) ( ) ( ) $.
Light Fixtures: ( ) ( ) ( ) $.
Walls and ceilings: ( ) ( ) ( ) $.
Windows: ( ) ( ) ( ) $.
Closets: ( ) ( ) ( ) $.
Other: ( ) ( ) ( ) $.
Other: ( ) ( ) ( ) $.

Bedroom 5

Doors and Locks: ( ) ( ) ( ) $.
Floor covering: ( ) ( ) ( ) $.
Light Fixtures: ( ) ( ) ( ) $.
Walls and ceilings: ( ) ( ) ( ) $.
Windows: ( ) ( ) ( ) $.
Closets: ( ) ( ) ( ) $.
Other: ( ) ( ) ( ) $.
Other: ( ) ( ) ( ) $.

Basement

Doors and Locks: ( ) ( ) ( ) $.
Floor covering: ( ) ( ) ( ) $.
Light Fixtures: ( ) ( ) ( ) $.
Walls and ceilings: ( ) ( ) ( ) $.
Windows: ( ) ( ) ( ) $.
Closets: ( ) ( ) ( ) $.
Other: ( ) ( ) ( ) $.
Other: ( ) ( ) ( )

Miscellaneous

Improvements _____

_____
_____
_____
_____
_____
_____
_____
_____
_____
_____
_____
_____
_____
_____

Budget Sheet

Category	How often	Monthly Income	Monthly Budget	Difference between the two
INCOME		$		
Wages Income		$		
Interest Income		$		
Bank Account Interest Income		$.		
INCOME SUBTOTAL		$		
EXPENSES				
Property Taxes				
Rent/Mortgages				
Utilities				
Groceries				
Clothing				
Shopping				
Entertainment				
Magazines				
Movies				
Concerts				
Car payments				
Savings				
Tax-deductibles				

Miscellaneous				
EXPENSES SUBTOTAL		$		
NET INCOME		$		

Car Auction Sheet

State _____ City _____

Address _____

Phone: ____-_____-_____

Email Address: _____

Date of Auction? _____

How many cars will be auctioned? _____

Description: _____ ( ) _____ ( )
_____ ( ) _____ ( )

_____ ( ) _____ ( )
_____ ( ) _____ ( )

How many are abandon? _____

How many has been seized by the police? _____

How many have been stolen? _____

How many have been took for parking tickets? _____

Are there tow trucks available for service? Yes_____ No_____

How much will the tow truck charge you to go to your destination? $_____

Can you drive off the impound lot without insurance? _____

Can you purchase temporary tags there? Yes_____ No_____

How long do you have to remove the car from the lot?

_____

If not remove in the time limit, how much money for the storage space a day? $_____ a day.

TRASHMAN CONTACT

Email: TheTrashmanisRich@Gmail.com

Facebook Page: Trashman Rich

Website: **WWW.JAVONTEJENNINGS.ACNIBO.COM**

Printed in the United States
By Bookmasters